First Questions and Answers about **Bugs**

How Far Can a Butterfly Fly?

TIME
LIFE for
Children®

ALEXANDRIA, VIRGINIA

Contents

Why are there so many bugs?

Everywhere you look, there are bugs! Crawling bugs. Flying bugs. Wiggling bugs. That's because insects can make homes in all kinds of places. They can live where it's very hot. They can live where there's hardly any food or water. Many bugs have hundreds of babies all at once, so new bugs are always being born everywhere.

The itsy–bitsy spider went up the waterspout!

Did you know?
People use the word "bug" to mean all sorts of little creatures that jump, creep, or fly around. Some of them, called "insects," have six legs and three body parts.

5

Are all ladybugs ladies?

No, they're not. Ladybugs may look alike, but some of them are girls and others are boys. Ladybugs are a kind of beetle. Some people say that a ladybug brings you good luck. Farmers like to have ladybugs around because they eat smaller bugs that hurt the farmers' plants.

Ladybug, ladybug, fly away home!

Did you know?
Some ladybugs have only two spots
on their wings. Others have as many as 15!

How far can a butterfly fly?

Some butterflies can go a very long way. They flap their wings to go fast, then glide to take a rest. Monarch butterflies travel the farthest. They don't like cold weather, so they fly all the way from Canada to Mexico for the winter. If you wanted to fly that far, you'd have to take a long airplane ride!

How do flies walk upside down?

A fly has a sticky pad at the end of each foot. With every step, the fly's foot sticks to the ceiling. Honeybees have sticky pads too, so they can walk up smooth glass or hang upside down from leaves or flowers.

Did you know?
A fly can taste things with its legs!
That's why it likes to land right
on top of your food.

How many legs do bugs have?

Most insects have six legs. But a spider, which is not an insect, has eight. It uses those extra legs to help it spin a web. Some bugs have even more legs than that—a lot more. A centipede usually has about 30 legs. A millipede can have more than 100!

Try it!
The next time you see a crawling bug, look at it closely. How many legs does it have? Does it use all of its legs to move?

Why do bugs have feelers?

Bugs don't have noses, so they pick up smells with their feelers instead. The smells help them figure out what's going on around them. An ant finds its way around by touching things with its feelers as it crawls. Whenever two ants meet, they touch their feelers together. They know from the smell if they come from the same nest.

Yum, chocolate!

Did you know?
A moth's feathery feelers can smell another moth far away. Mosquitoes use their feelers to hear sounds.

How come ants always find our picnic?

There are many, many ants outside. No matter where you have a picnic, the chances are good that ants are nearby. Some ants are always on the lookout for food. When they find it, they take it back to their nest. If the food is too heavy to move, they get more ants to help them carry it.

Where's my cookie?

Did you know?
Different ants like different kinds of food.
Some ants look only for sweet foods,
like sugar. Other ants like greasy foods,
such as potato chips.

Why is that bug sitting so still?

It's waiting for its next meal! A praying mantis sits quietly on a plant, watching other bugs come and go. When a butterfly or a caterpillar gets too close, the mantis grabs it with its long, strong front legs and eats it.

A green praying mantis looks just like a leaf. A brown praying mantis looks just like a stick. These colors help the mantis stay hidden until it catches another bug to eat.

Did you know?
A praying mantis can attack a hummingbird,
a tiny mouse, or a small garter snake! It is
the only bug that can turn its head like a human.

How do bugs hide?

Many bugs are hard to see. Their colors and shapes make them look like the plants around them. Hiding keeps these bugs safe from animals and other bugs that want to eat them. Can you find six bugs hiding here?

Some **butterflies** resemble leaves.

Bright green **katydids** are hard to spot in the grass.

This **moth** is hard to see on the bark of a tree.

Ready or not, here I come!

A **stick insect** looks just like a twig.

Treehoppers look like sharp thorns. No wonder animals stay away from them!

When an **inchworm** caterpillar stands still, animals think it is only a tree branch.

21

How else do bugs stay safe?

Yikes!

This **butterfly** has spots on its wings that look like big eyes. The spots may scare away birds that might hurt it.

A **ladybug's** legs give off a bad-tasting liquid. Yuck!

Does this look like a stinging bee?
It's not! Its really a kind of fly,
called a **flower fly**. It fools animals
into thinking it can sting them.

Bombardier beetles give off
a smelly gas—just like a skunk!

A **click beetle** lies on its back and
pretends to be dead. Then, with a
loud "click," it flips right side up
and runs away!

23

Why do honeybees sting?

Honeybees sting to protect themselves and their homes from enemies. If you stay away from honeybees, they will stay away from you. The sting of a honeybee hurts, but it's even worse for the honeybee. After it stings someone or something, the honeybee loses its stinger and dies.

Why do bees make honey?

Honey is the food that bees eat. Bees make honey from a sweet liquid in flowers called nectar.

First, a bee lands on a flower. Using its long, tube-shaped tongue, it sucks out the nectar.

Next, the bee flies back to the hive with the nectar. It makes many trips a day.

Finally, other bees in the hive help turn the nectar into honey.

Did you know?
When a bee finds flowers, it does a special dance that tells the other bees in the hive where the flowers are.

What do other insects eat?

Practically everything!

Moths and **butterflies** use their tongues to drink nectar. Their tongues are longer than bees' tongues, so they can reach deeper inside flowers.

Lots of bugs, including **dragonflies**, eat other bugs.

Hey–what about me?

Caterpillars and **katydids** chew leaves.

Horseflies bite animals and sip their blood.

Termites eat wood. So do some **ants** and **beetles.**

How does a spider catch its food?

A spider builds a web to trap the insects it likes to eat. These may be anything from moths to grasshoppers to flies. Some webs have sticky threads that the spider makes inside its body. When a bug lands on the web, its legs get caught in these threads. Other webs aren't sticky at all–they're just so full of twists and turns that the bug can't find its way out.

Did you know?
The spider doesn't get stuck because it knows just where the sticky threads are.

Come into my parlor!

Try it!
Spider webs have different shapes. Some look like circles. Others look like triangles. A few are just wispy lines. How many different spiderwebs can you find outside?

Why does a mosquito bite itch?

When a mosquito bites you, it puts some liquid under your skin. This liquid makes it easier for the mosquito to drink blood. But it also makes the bite itch.

How can grasshoppers jump so far?

Because they have such strong muscles in their back legs! These muscles provide the power for their long-distance leaps through the grass where they live.

Did you know?
Tiny fleas are the world's best insect jumpers.
They use their powerful legs to jump a foot
in the air, which is 300 times their own length!

What do baby bugs look like?

Some baby bugs look like their mothers or fathers.
Young spiders, crickets, and grasshoppers all look
like their parents. But other baby bugs, called larvae,
look quite different.

Baby butterflies look different from their parents, too.
When a butterfly egg hatches, a tiny caterpillar crawls
out. The caterpillar will turn into a butterfly later on.

Mosquito larvae
live in water.

Ladybug larvae are dark
bugs with soft bodies.

Do bugs talk to each other?

All the time! But bugs use sounds, not words, to tell each other things. Some bugs make sounds to let other bugs know they are there. That's one way male bugs attract females. Other sounds mean danger is near. A few bugs make sounds to scare away their enemies.

Grasshoppers rub their back legs against their wings to make sounds.

Male **cicadas** make loud sounds
by vibrating the sides of their bodies.

Male **crickets** chirp to females
by rubbing their wings together.

Why do moths fly around lights?

Most moths come out at night. They use the light of the moon to find their way around. But when a moth sees a light, it thinks it is the moon. The confused bug flies around the light instead.

Try it!

Turn on a porch light on a summer night. Do moths fly around it? Check around the light the next morning. You may find some moths resting nearby.

What's the biggest bug of all?

Most people think of bugs as tiny creatures, but some insects are really quite large.

The longest bug is the giant **stick insect**. With its legs out, it is almost as long as your arm!

The **Atlas moth** has wings that are larger than those of many birds.

The **Queen Alexandra Birdwing butterfly** is one of the biggest butterflies. From wing to wing it is a little longer than a pencil.

The **Goliath beetle** weighs more than any other insect. It can be as heavy as a candy bar.

Why don't I see bugs in winter?

For most bugs, it's just too cold to stay outside! Many bugs sleep through the winter. Honeybees rest in their hives. Ants sleep in their nests.

Isabella moths pass the winter as woolly bear caterpillars.

A **luna moth** spends the winter in a cocoon.

A **cabbage white butterfly** grows inside a case called a chrysalis.

Ladybugs snooze together in piles of leaves or underneath the bark of trees.

Praying mantis eggs stay in egg cases through the winter. They will hatch in the spring.

A few bugs do come out in winter. **Snow fleas** look like tiny grains of black pepper hopping around in the snow.

Do bugs help people?

Yes, all the time. Bugs help plants and flowers reproduce. They give us honey to eat and silk for making clothes. They are food for fish, birds, and other animals. Insects recycle the food we throw away, and they keep the soil rich. We couldn't live without bugs!

Sleep tight! Don't let the bedbugs bite!

Did you know?
There are more insects in the world than any other kind of animal.

47

TIME-LIFE for CHILDREN ®
Managing Editor: Patricia Daniels
Editorial Directors: Jean Burke Crawford, Allan Fallow,
Karin Kinney, Sara Mark
Senior Art Director: Susan White
Editorial Coordinator: Marike van der Veen
Administrative Assistant: Mary M. Saxton
Production Manager: Marlene Zack
Senior Copyeditor: Colette Stockum
Production: Celia Beattie
Supervisor of Quality Control: James King
Assistant Supervisor of Quality Control: Miriam Newton
Library: Louise D. Forstall, Anne Heising

Special Contributor: Barbara Klein
Researcher: Jocelyn Lindsay
Writer: Andrew Gutelle

Designed by: **David Bennett Books Ltd**

Series design: David Bennett
Book design: David Bennett
Art direction: David Bennett
Illustrated by: Michael Brownlow
Additional cover
illustrations by: Nick Baxter

First printing. Printed in U.S.A.
Published simultaneously in Canada.

Time Life Inc. is a wholly owned subsidiary of THE TIME INC. BOOK COMPANY.

TIME-LIFE is a trademark of Time Warner Inc. U.S.A.

For subscription information, call 1-800-621-7026.

School and library distribution by Time-Life Education,P.O. Box 85026, Richmond, VA 23285-5026.

Library of Congress Cataloging-in-Publication Data
How far can a butterfly fly? : first questions and answers about bugs.
p. cm. (Time -Life library of first questions and answers)
ISBN 0-7835-0882-4 (hardcover). ISBN 0-7835-0883-2 (1lb.bdg.)
1. Insects Miscellanea Juvenile literature. [1. Insects-Miscellanea. 2. Questions and answers.]
I. Time-Life for Children (Firm) II. Series: Library of first questions and answers.
QL467.2.H695 1994
595.7—dc20
94-4688
CIP
AC

Consultants

Dr. Lewis P. Lipsitt, an internationally recognized specialist on childhood development, was the 1990 recipient of the Nicholas Hobbs Award for science in the service of children. He has served as the science director for the American Psychological Association and is a professor of psychology and medical science at Brown University, where he directed the Child Study Center from 1968 to 1993.

Dr. Judith A. Schickedanz, an authority on the education of preschool children, is an associate professor of early childhood education at the Boston University School of Education, where she also directs the Early Childhood Learning Laboratory. Her published work includes *More Than the ABC's: Early Stages of Reading and Writing Development* as well as several textbooks and many scholarly papers.

Carol Anelli Sheppard, a research associate at the National Institutes of Health, received advanced degrees in Entomology from the University of Illinois, where she studied the physiology of blow flies and gypsy moths. Her fascination with insects began as a child when she raised monarch and black-swallowtail caterpillars.

W. Steve Sheppard, studies the population genetics and evolutionary biology of honey bees and other insects at the United States Department of Agriculture-ARS Bee Research Laboratory. His interest in entomology got its start in childhood when he investigated old beekeeping equipment stored in his great grandmother's garage.